First published in Great Britain 2019
by Red Shed, an imprint of Egmont UK Limited,
The Yellow Building, 1 Nicholas Road, London W11 4AN

www.egmont.co.uk

Text copyright © Egmont UK Ltd 2019
Illustrations copyright © Lara Hawthorne 2019

ISBN 978 1 4052 9421 8

A CIP catalogue record for this title is available from the British Library.

HIDDEN ADVENTURES

LARA HAWTHORNE

RED SHED

6 sandals

Some of the soles of Tutankhamun's sandals were painted with captured enemies so he could walk all over them!

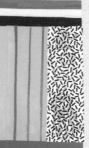

5 senet board games

Senet board games were found but no one knows the exact rules for this popular ancient Egyptian game.

8 fruit baskets

Hidden in the tomb were baskets containing 3,000-year-old doums (sweet orange-red fruits).

3 model boats

Wooden model boats were buried in the tomb so that Tutankhamun could use them in the afterlife.

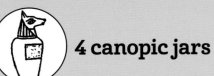

4 canopic jars

Canopic jars were found. Each contained one of the king's internal organs: stomach, intestines, lungs and liver.

1 headrest

Headrests were used instead of a pillow – the neck rested on the curve.

Over 5,000 treasures were found in King Tutankhamun's Egyptian tomb when it was discovered in 1922. Use your red lens to reveal some of these incredible finds.

And there are more treasures from all over the world just waiting to be found – sometimes in the most unusual places . . .

Dive down deep below the
ocean waves to reveal
a treasure trove of wonders.

The oceans are home to around 3 million shipwrecks.

10 gold bars

There were 125 gold bars discovered on the *Nuestra Señora de Atocha* wreck, part of its £340 million treasure.

7 anchors

An anchor thought to be from one of Columbus' ships weighed over 545kg (heavier than 6 baby elephants!).

1 ring

Amongst the 19,000 objects recovered from the *Mary Rose* shipwreck was a silver ring with a 'K' on it.

8 silver coins

Chests of Spanish silver dollars were found on the *San José* – a ship that sank in 1708 in the Caribbean Sea.

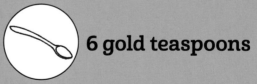

6 gold teaspoons

Gold teaspoons were among 5,500 objects that were discovered on the *Titanic*, which sank in 1912.

5 motorbikes

The SS *Thistlegorm* had motorbikes, trains and trucks on board when it sank in 1941.

3 giant spiders

Goliath bird-eating spiders are huge tarantulas that live in silk-lined burrows in South America.

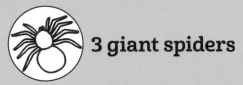
6 rafflesia flowers

These are the world's largest flowers and are found in Southeast Asia. They smell like rotting meat!

9 glass knives

Archaeologists found knives made from volcanic glass in a royal tomb in the Mayan city of Xunantunich, Belize.

4 planes

When lightning struck a plane over Peru, 17-year-old Juliane Koepcke survived a 3-km fall from the sky.

7 horned tree agamids

The Phuket horned tree agamid was among 163 new species found in Southeast Asia in 2015.

4 Olmec colossal heads

These mysterious giant stone heads were made by the ancient Olmec civilization in Mexico.

Peep through the trees, deep in the heart of the jungle, and uncover some amazing animals, plants and extraordinary items.

More than half of the world's plants
and animals live in jungles.

Hike up to the top of the mountain and keep an eye out for some unexpected objects and creatures along the way.

Peaking at 8,848m, Mount Everest is the world's highest mountain.

10 bags of rubbish

There are tonnes of rubbish on top of Mount Everest that have been left behind by the climbers who hike to the summit each year.

3 mountain goats

These animals can be found in mountains in North America. They aren't true goats – just close relatives.

8 Yeti footprints

The Yeti has been part of Himalayan legend for centuries. So far no one has proved it exists but perhaps it hasn't been found yet?

5 marine fossils

Fossils of sea creatures were found in Mount Everest's rocks in 1924 – they proved the mountain used to be below sea level.

1 church organ

An organ was found on the top of Ben Nevis in 2006. It is thought to have been carried up there in 1971 to raise money for charity.

6 jewels

An explorer found a box on Mont Blanc, containing emeralds, rubies and sapphires – estimated to be worth over £193,000.

Brave the heat of the scorching
desert and journey over the dunes
to reveal some surprises . . .

The welwitschia plant can live up to
1,500 years and it is only found in
one part of the Namibian desert.

5 thorny devils

These spiky lizards are able to change colour and can inflate themselves, looking bigger to scare off predators.

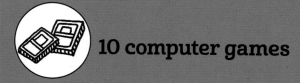

1 giant hand

Part of a huge cement hand sculpted by Mario Irarrázabal pokes up through the sand of the Atacama desert, Chile.

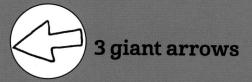

10 computer games

A computer company buried leftover games in the deserts in New Mexico. They were found in 2014 and sold on eBay.

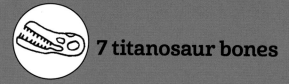

3 giant arrows

In deserts across America, stone arrows, each about 20m long, helped planes navigate to deliver mail in the 1920s.

7 titanosaur bones

Bones of the largest-known dinosaur were found in the Patagonian desert in 2012. This dino was up to 40m long.

4 Nazca lines

These mysterious drawings in the sand by Peruvian people over 1,500 years ago can only be seen properly from the air.

1 lake

It took 20 years of drilling to reach Lake Vostok, hidden almost 4km under the ice. Scientists broke through in 2012.

5 tins of food

Tins of preserved food and a 100-year-old fruitcake were discovered in a hut used by British explorer Captain Robert Scott.

7 notebooks

A notebook from the Scott expedition of 1911, belonging to George Murray Levick, was found in the ice in 2014.

8 paintings

A 118-year-old painting by explorer Dr Edward Wilson was found in 2017, hidden by penguin poo and tin cans!

14 icefish

In 1928, zoologist Ditlef Rustad discovered a fish with transparent blood. A chemical in its blood stops it freezing, so it can survive the cold conditions.

1 mountain

Russian explorers discovered the Gamburtsev Mountains in 1958. They were buried under 5km of ice.

Brrrr! Are you ready for a chilly adventure in the icy Antarctic polar desert to uncover some frozen treasures?

Antarctica was the very last continent to be discovered. If all of the ice here melted, the world's oceans would rise by about 50–65m.

Journey into the glowing cave
for an underground adventure.
What can you find?

The world's largest cave system is Hang Son Doong in Vietnam – it's so big that a Boeing 747 plane could fit in its largest cavern!

8 glow-worms

They aren't actually worms at all! They are fungus gnats – flies that feed on fungi.

6 olms

These eyeless salamanders live in the water in complete darkness and can survive for up to 100 years.

10 bats

Bracken Cave in Texas is home to about 15 million bats. Every year, in March, they fly here from Mexico.

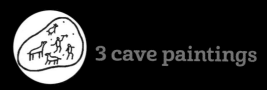

3 cave paintings

Cave paintings in Lascaux, France, are about 17,000 years old. They show horses and other animals and figures.

5 shell necklaces

Shell beads were found in Blombos Cave, South Africa. They belonged to humans who lived over 76,000 years ago.

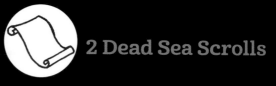

2 Dead Sea Scrolls

The remains of up to 900 ancient manuscripts, mostly religious writings, were found in the Qumran caves, Israel.

1 underground city

In 1963, a man knocked down a wall in his home in Turkey and found an old city, Derinkuyu, once home to 20,000 people.

9 bones

Catacombs in Paris contain the remains of millions of people, moved there over 12 years from 1786 from Paris cemeteries.

4 ships

Some parts of San Francisco are built on top of abandoned ships used in the California Gold Rush, 1848–1855.

8 footprints

When the 4th century port of Theodosius in Istanbul was uncovered in 2011, 8,000-year-old footprints were found.

1 train track

Franklin D. Roosevelt used a secret train track at Grand Central Terminal, New York, to access the Waldorf Astoria Hotel.

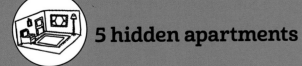

5 hidden apartments

When the Eiffel Tower opened in Paris, in 1889, designer Gustave Eiffel revealed he had built an apartment near the top.

Explore the bustling city and uncover secret places and treasures below its surface.

The number 4 is thought to be unlucky
in some Asian countries, so many buildings
don't have a fourth floor.

Peek inside the different rooms to discover some surprising gems.

Lena Paahlsson found her wedding ring one day on a carrot she pulled up in her garden – she had lost it 16 years before!

1 comic book

A 1938 comic book used to insulate a wall in a house in Minnesota, USA, sold for around £130,000.

3 treasure chests

Over 200 rings, brooches, belt buckles and silver plates that were over 650 years old were found in a garden in Austria in 2007.

2 cars

A Ferrari Dino 246 GTS was discovered in a garden by two boys in 1978, in Los Angeles, USA. It was then sold at auction to a mechanic.

7 skulls

Some scientists believe that a skull found in an attic in France in 2008 belongs to King Henry IV. Though others aren't so sure.

5 love letters

A love letter from 1944 was found in the wall of a Massachusetts, USA, home during renovations in 2017.

1 meteorite

A professor in the US discovered that the rock he used as a doorstop for over 30 years was actually a meteorite worth $100,000.

4 Laotian rock rats

Discovered in 2005, this ancient rat belongs to a family that was thought to have been extinct for 11 million years!

7 Chinese bowls

A white bowl bought at a US garage sale for $3 turned out to be a 1,000-year-old treasure that later sold for $2.2 million.

1 Declaration of Independence

Hidden behind a painting bought for $4 at a US market was a copy of this historic document. It later sold for $2.42 million.

5 diamond rings

Bought in the 1980s for £10 at a car boot sale, a gigantic diamond ring was sold in 2017 for over £656,750!

3 snail-eating turtles

A new type of snail-eating turtle was discovered by accident in a Thailand food market in 2016.

2 watches

A watch worn in a James Bond film was bought in 2013 for £25 and sold in 2017 at auction for over £103,875!

Wander through the busy market brimming with riches. Look closely, some are more extraordinary than they first appear to be . . .

With over 4,000 shops, the Grand Bazaar in Istanbul is one of the world's biggest covered markets.

Look high up into the starry sky to see the luminous Moon and reveal hidden objects whizzing around above Earth.

There are over 100 human-made objects on the Moon – many of them were left behind by space missions between 1969 and 1972.

4 pizzas

In 2001, a pizza was sent to Russian cosmonaut Yuri Usachov while he was on the International Space Station (ISS).

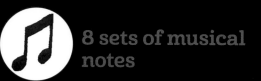
8 sets of musical notes

A Beatles song, 'Across the Universe', was beamed into space in 2008. It travelled at 300,000 km/second.

6 gloves

During a spacewalk in 1965, Ed White let go of a glove. It orbited Earth for a month, then burnt up in Earth's atmosphere.

3 family photos

Astronaut Charles Duke left a photo of his family on the Moon in 1972. It is still there – though probably completely faded.

5 plants

Vegetables, such as lettuce and peas, have been grown on the ISS as part of the astronauts' 'space garden'.

2 tool bags

Heide Stefanyshyn-Piper dropped her toolbag during a spacewalk in 2008 – it contained over £75,000 worth of tools.

The adventure isn't over yet! Travel back through the book and use the lens to find some more hidden treasures and discoveries . . .

 1 keg of butter

Bog butters are often found in Ireland but one of the largest discoveries was in 2013 when a 5,000-year-old wooden keg of butter weighing 45kg was dug up.

 4 Terracotta Army pieces

When a group of farmers were digging a water well in 1974 they uncovered the tomb of Qin Shi Huang, China's first emperor. Guarding his tomb for over 2,000 years were thousands of life-size clay soldiers and horses.

 1 time capsule

In 1795, a time capsule was buried below the Massachusetts State House, USA, by founding fathers Samuel Adams and Paul Revere. When it was dug up and opened, it revealed silver coins, newspapers, and a bronze medal of the first US president, George Washington.

 **2 bowling balls**

Since work began in 2009 on the construction of London's Elizabeth line railway, more than 10,000 archaeological objects have been discovered. These include a wooden Tudor bowling ball and medieval ice skates.

 2 worms

In 2011, a new type of worm was discovered 3.6km below the earth in a gold mine in South Africa. This 'devil worm' (*Halicephalobus mephisto*) is one of the deepest-living animals.

3 loaves of bread

A 2,000-year-old loaf of bread was discovered in an oven during an excavation of Herculaneum in Italy. It had been there since the city was covered in ash during the volcanic eruption of Mount Vesuvius in 79CE. The loaf had the baker's name stamped onto it: Celer, slave of Quintus Granius Verus.

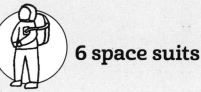

6 space suits

In 2017, college students discovered 6 NASA space suits in a charity shop in Florida. They paid less than £1 for all the suits worn in the 1980s by astronauts including George Nelson, Robert A. Parker and Charles D. Walker, even though they are worth thousands of pounds.

1 book

A 15th-century text called 'The Voynich Manuscript' first appeared in records in the 16th century and travelled around Europe until it disappeared for 250 years. In 1912, it was bought by Wilfrid Voynich. It is written in an unknown alphabet – people are still trying to find out what it says.

And can you find the family of mice in every scene?